Black Widows

Black Widows

The Child's World

Published in the United States of America by The Child's World®
PO Box 326
Chanhassen, MN 55317-0326
800-599-READ
www.childsworld.com

Project Manager Mary Berendes
Editor Katherine Stevenson, Ph.D.
Designer Mary Berendes
**Our sincere thanks to Robert Mitchell, Ph.D.,
for his input and guidance on this book.**

Photo Credits
ANIMALS ANIMALS © Bill Beatty: 2
ANIMALS ANIMALS © Doug Wechsler: 20 (main)
ANIMALS ANIMALS © G. W. Willis: 9
ANIMALS ANIMALS © James H. Robinson: 16, 20 (inset)
ANIMALS ANIMALS © Richard Shiell: 29
ANIMALS ANIMALS © TC Nature: 10, 15, 19
© 1996 Anthony Mercieca/Dembinsky Photo Assoc. Inc.: 6
© Bill Johnson: 13
© Brian Kenney: cover
© Karen Tweedy-Holmes/CORBIS: 30
© Robert & Linda Mitchell: 23, 24, 26

Library of Congress Cataloging-in-Publication Data
Murray, Peter, 1952 Sept. 29–
Black widows / by Peter Murray.
p. cm.
ISBN 1-56766-977-8 (lib. bdg. : alk. paper)
1. Black widow spider—Juvenile literature.
[1. Black widow spider. 2. Spiders.] I. Title.
QL458.42.T54 M87 2003
595.4'4—dc21
2001000302

On the cover...

Front cover: You can clearly see the hourglass shape on this female black widow's belly.
Page 2: This female black widow spider is spinning a new web.

Table of Contents

The attic is dark and dusty and full of cobwebs. Some of the cobwebs have a neat pattern to them. Others have lines that go every which way. A spider sits in the middle of one of the messy cobwebs. The spider is black and shiny and small. It is also very dangerous! What is this deadly spider? It's a black widow.

← This female black widow's web is in a tangled shape.

Where Do Black Widows Live?

Black widows live in every state except Alaska. In some southern states, they are one of the most common spiders. They often make their tangled webs in wood piles, under rocks, or in other places where they aren't likely to be bothered. Most black widows that make their homes indoors live in dark corners. Unless you are looking for them, you might never know they are there.

If you find the web of a black widow, the spider will probably be hiding at the back. That's because the spider is shy and wants to be left alone. Don't disturb its web! Black widows don't like to be bothered.

This female black widow lives in an Arizona canyon. ⇒

What Do Black Widows Look Like?

Male and female black widows look very different. Females have a shiny black body about the size of a large pea. They also have a reddish orange, hourglass-shaped spot on their belly. Male black widows are only about half the size of the females. They have red or white stripes on their back.

Black widows have fangs that shoot poison, or **venom**, into the animals they eat. The venom makes the animal, or **prey**, unable to move. The venom keeps the meal from getting away before the spider is ready to eat.

This male black widow is walking on a log in Maryland. ⇒

What Do Black Widows Eat?

Black widows eat insects. The spider waits for its prey to get caught in its sticky web. The spider feels the tiny movements, or **vibrations**, as the insect struggles to get free. The black widow runs to the insect and spins a layer of silk over it. Then it bites the insect to shoot venom into its body. Now the spider is ready to eat. After sucking the insect dry, the black widow cuts it loose from its web. The dry "shell" of the dead insect falls to the ground.

A female black widow usually spends her entire life in one place. She lives for about a year. The ground under the web of a full-grown female is littered with dead insects. One black widow spider scientists studied ate 255 flies, two crickets, and a caterpillar!

This female is feeding on an ant she trapped in her web. ⇒

The male black widow lives for only a few months. As soon as he is full grown, he leaves his web in search of a mate. When he finds the web of a female black widow, he approaches very, very carefully. He touches the female's web and makes it vibrate. If the female returns the vibrations, she is ready to mate. If the female is not ready to mate, she might eat the male for lunch!

⇐ Here you can see how different male and female black widows look. The female is much larger.

If he isn't chased away, the male moves onto the web. After the spiders mate, the male leaves the web quickly. If he is not quick enough, he might become the female's next meal. That is why these spiders are called black widows (a widow is a woman whose husband is dead). Sometimes the male brings the female an insect wrapped in silk. If the female accepts the gift, she will not be so hungry. She might even let him stay in her web for a few days.

This male and female are getting ready to mate. ⇒

How Are Baby Black Widows Born?

After mating, the female black widow makes a silk pouch called an **egg sac**. The sac is about as big as her body. She fills the sac with 200 or 300 bright yellow eggs. Each egg will develop into a baby spider, or **spiderling**.

After the black widow lays all her eggs, she spins a silky covering for the sac and attaches it to her web. The black widow stays near the sac to protect her eggs from danger. This is not a good time to go near her web!

⇐ *Main photo*: This female is guarding her egg sacs.

Small photo: This picture shows all the tiny eggs inside an egg sac.

What Are Baby Black Widows Like?

A few weeks later, a hole appears in each egg sac, and the spiderlings start to come out. The young spiders are clear and rubbery, with no markings. They swarm out of the egg sac and fill the web. The mother black widow watches her babies. If she is hungry, she will eat a few of them. The baby spiders are hungry, too—sometimes they even eat each other!

This female is guarding her babies as they ⇒
crawl out of the hole in their egg sac.

The spiderlings soon leave their mother's web. Some crawl off to the nearest dark corner and build their own webs. But most find their way to the top of a plant, a fence post, or some other high place. They use their spinnerets to spin long, light strands of silk. The wind catches each silky strand and lifts the spider up into the air. The moving air carries each spider far away. This way of moving is called **ballooning**. When the spider lands, it finds a dark corner where it will build its first web.

⇐ These older spiderlings are in danger of being eaten by their mother if she gets hungry enough.

Each spiderling grows quickly. Every week or two, the young spider gets too big for its hard, shell-like skin. It hangs from a strand of silk and bends its body until its skin splits. Then it wriggles out of its old skin. The baby black widow will **molt,** or shed its old skin, several times before reaching its full size.

The first time a black widow molts, it is light gray or yellow with an orange abdomen. With each new skin, the spider gets darker. After the last molt, the spider has its adult colors.

⇐ These older black widow spiderlings are
almost ready to find their own webs.

How Dangerous Are Black Widows?

Male black widows are harmless to humans, but females are much more dangerous. In fact, the female's venom is so strong that just one bite can make a person very sick. Most people who are bitten recover, but some have died from the bite of a black widow.

This female has built her web in a ⇒
quiet corner of a California home.

Some people think that black widow spiders are fierce, bad-tempered creatures that should be killed. The truth is, black widows are shy spiders that don't bite people unless they are bothered. All spiders help us by keeping other insects under control. Black widows usually build their webs in out-of-the-way places. But that doesn't mean you should let a black widow live under your bed! These spiders might be small, but they're dangerous. You don't want to mess with the black widow spider!

⇐ This female black widow spider is spinning her web at Zion National Park in Utah.

Glossary

abdomen (AB-doh-men)
The back half of a spider's body is called the abdomen. Its abdomen contains organs that spin silk.

arachnids (uh-RAK-nids)
Arachnids are animals that have eight legs and a body that is divided into two areas. Black widows and other spiders are arachnids, and so are ticks and scorpions.

ballooning (buh-LOO-ning)
Young spiders move to new locations by drifting on the wind, or ballooning. They stand on a high place, spin a long strand of silk, and let the wind carry them away.

cephalothorax (seh-fuh-loh-THOR-ax)
A cephalothorax is the front body area of an arachnid. A black widow's cephalothorax contains its eyes, mouth, fangs, and stomach.

egg sac (EGG SAK)
A baglike egg sac is where a female black widow places her eggs. The baby spiders leave the egg sac after they hatch.

molt (MOLT)
When an animal molts, it sheds its outer layer of skin, fur, or feathers. Growing black widows molt by shedding their outgrown skins.

prey (PRAY)
Animals that are eaten by other animals are called prey. Insects are prey for black widows.

spiderling (SPY-der-ling)
A spiderling is a baby spider. Black widow spiderlings are sometimes eaten by their mother.

spinnerets (spin-ner-ETZ)
A spider's spinnerets are the parts of its body that produce silk. A black widow's spinnerets are on the very tip of its abdomen.

venom (VEN-um)
Venom is the poison some animals make in their bodies. Female black widows have very powerful venom.

vibrations (vy-BRAY-shunz)
Vibrations are very tiny movements. Black widows feel the vibrations caused by insects caught in their webs.

Index

Web Sites

Visit our homepage for lots of links about black widow spiders!
http://www.childsworld.com/links.html

Note to Parents, Teachers, and Librarians:
We routinely verify our Web links to make sure they're safe, active sites—
so encourage your readers to check them out!